READING
THE
SPORTS
PAGE

READING THE SPORTS PAGE: A Guide to Understanding Sports Statistics

A Skillbook

Jeremy R. Feinberg

New Discovery Books • *New York*
Maxwell Macmillan Canada • *Toronto*
Maxwell Macmillan International
New York   Oxford   Singapore   Sydney

New Discovery Books
Macmillan Publishing Company
866 Third Avenue
New York, NY 10022

Maxwell Macmillan Canada. Inc.
1200 Eglinton Avenue East
Suite 200
Don Mills, Ontario M3C 3N1

Macmillan Publishing Company is part of the Maxwell Communications Group of Companies.

First Edition

Printed in the United States of America

10 9 8 7 6 5 4 3 2 1

Library of Congress Cataloging-in-Publication Data
Feinberg, Jeremy R.
     Reading the sports page: a guide to understanding sports statistics/by Jeremy R. Feinberg—1st ed.
     p.   cm.
     Includes index.
     ISBN 0-02-734420-7
     1. Sports—statistical methods. 2. Newspapers—Sections, columns, etc.—Sports. I. Title
GV741.F43 1992
796'.021—dc20   92-18972

Dedication

To Jack Rohan, Richard Gersten, David Dunkel, Allan Boyers, and Gerald Feinberg—five men who, at different times and in very different ways, have all enhanced my love for and knowledge of the world of sports.

Acknowledgments

I would like to thank the following people for their research assistance: Michael Neft and David Neft from the Society of American Baseball Research, Elizabeth Berke, Stephanie Geosits and Elliot Regenstein from the *Columbia Daily Spectator;* Doug Feinberg, Jeff Saperstein, Ben Lawsky, and Alex Oberweger.

I would also like to thank Lawrence Van Gelder, Roger Jackson, and Paul Kuharsky for molding me as a writer; Kris Kanthak and my parents, Barbara and Gerald Feinberg, for their editorial assistance; and Quaifferlee Van Benschoten for general support.

CONTENTS

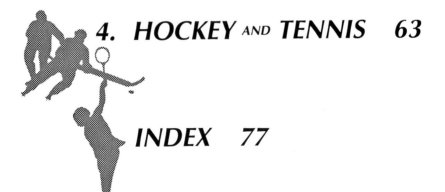

Introduction

You just can't escape them.

You run into them when you watch sports on television, read about a game in the newspaper, or sit in the stands rooting for your favorite team. Sports statistics, otherwise known as **stats,** are everywhere. As long as games have been played and people have kept score, stats have been around. Today they are a very important part of the world of sports. In fact, at athletic events across the country, there are often more people keeping stats during the game than there are referees, players, and coaches!

Because sports statistics are so important, most newspapers devote an entire page, called an **agate page,** to listing sports stats. Some papers may even have two or three agate pages. Serious sports fans often turn to the agate page first to check the statistics before reading the stories about the games.

People often think of statistics simply as collections of numbers. In fact, that is what they started out as. *State-istics,* as they were first called, consisted of information gathered about the populations of different areas around the world. State-istics were used to tell how many people lived in a given place and what areas were growing the most quickly.

Today in sports, people use stats for similar reasons. They study the various types of statistics to see which teams are the best and worst, which players are improving, and who has the best record. Different types of stats and records are constantly being developed as people try to discover new ways to measure the success of players and teams.

So what's the big deal? Why do so many coaches keep track of and study their own and other teams' stats? Why are dozens of different statistical charts, graphs, and tables flashed on the television screen during games? Why are stats found on the backs of sports trading cards? Why is there a separate section for sports stats in the newspaper? And, most of all, what do all these stats tell us?

Stats help us do several things. First, they let us compare different players and teams over a period of time. For example, stats can help answer the question: Who is a better basketball player, Chicago Bulls guard Michael Jordan or Philadelphia 76ers forward Charles Barkley? They can also give us an idea of how current players compare to players from years past. By examining their career statistics, for example, we can find out how the current New York Yankees' first baseman Don Mattingly compares to Lou Gehrig, the Yankees' first baseman during the 1920s and 1930s.

Because stats give so much information about how well a player or team has performed in the past, they can also help predict future performance. This is why newspaper reporters, television sportscasters, coaches, and fans pay close attention to the stats. By looking at the numbers, they can try to determine what is going to happen before a game even begins, comment more accurately on what happens during a game, and explain what actually did happen and why when the game is over. It's a lot easier for the morning papers' football columnists to write about how Houston Oilers quarterback Warren Moon picked apart the Philadelphia Eagles' defense if they have statistics to back them up.

Another useful thing that statistics do is help us figure

out the best and worst performances of all time. They let us keep track of world and local records so that we know when one has been broken. When an old record is broken or is in danger of being broken, reporters and broadcasters give a lot of coverage to it.

For example, for 57 years Ty Cobb was credited with having the most career hits by a baseball player. In 1985, when Pete Rose was coming close to beating Cobb's feat, many newspapers ran a daily "Pete Rose hit watch" to chart his progress. Eventually Rose broke the record.

STANDINGS

While there are different kinds of statistics for different sports, there are two basic stats that every sport has: wins and losses. At the end of the playing season in any given sport, the team with the most number of victories is considered the best in the sport. Wins and losses are used to determine which team wins a title, goes to the playoffs, or is the champion for a given season.

Every day during the season, newspapers publish team **standings** in a given sport. All the teams in a particular sport are ranked according to how well they are doing, based on their wins and losses. Next to each team you will see columns marked **W,** for wins, and **L,** for losses.

The diagram on page 14 shows team standings in baseball's American League on an average day. There are two separate leagues in baseball, so there are separate standings for both the American and National leagues. Each league also has two divisions, and these are also listed separately. From the chart we can see that in the Eastern Division of the American League, the Toronto Blue Jays are in first place, with 12 wins and 3 losses. The Oakland A's are leading in the Western Division, with 10 wins and 4 losses.

Listed to the right of the team's wins and losses is its

American League

East Division

	W	L	Pct.	GB
Toronto	12	3	.800	--
Yankees	9	5	.643	2½
Baltimore	8	5	.615	3
Boston	6	6	.500	4½
Milwaukee	5	7	.417	5½
Cleveland	5	10	.333	7
Detroit	4	11	.267	8

West Division

	W	L	Pct.	GB
Oakland	10	4	.714	--
Chicago	8	5	.615	1½
Texas	9	6	.600	1½
California	7	6	.538	2½
Seattle	7	7	.500	3
Minnesota	4	8	.333	5
Kansas City	1	12	.077	8½

winning percentage. A winning percentage tells you how often a team wins. It is used to compare teams that might not have played the same number of games. For instance, if the Boston Red Sox have played 26 games and the Seattle Mariners have only played 24, we can still compare them using each team's winning percentage.

To find a team's winning percentage, we add up the number of wins and losses a team has and divide that number into the number of wins it has had. In the case of the New York Yankees in the diagram, we add the number of wins (9) and the number of losses (5) to get the total number of games played (14). If we divide that into the number of wins (9) we get a winning percentage of .643.

The winning percentage can also be thought of as the number of games a team would be expected to win if it played 1,000 games. For instance, if the Yankees played 1,000 games, they would be expected to win 643 of them.

The higher a team's winning percentage, the better it is doing in the standings. Most papers list the different teams in a sport in order of their winning percentage. Now when you hear announcers and reporters say that one team is ahead of another "by percentage points," you'll know what they mean.

Farther to the right of the winning percentage column you sometimes find a column labeled **GB.** This is the **games behind** column. The numbers in the GB column tells you how far behind a sport's leading team the other teams are. You'll notice that the lower a team's winning percentage, the more games behind the leader it is. In the example we have used, the Chicago White Sox are in second place in the American League's Western Division. They are 1½ games behind the leaders, the Oakland A's. The GB number changes depending on who a team plays and who the team they are trying to catch up to plays.

If the standings you are reading do not have a games behind column, you can easily find out the information. To figure out how many games behind the leader your favorite team is, all you need to do is add and subtract. The team in first place is called the **leader.** The team you want to compute games behind for is called the **trailer.**

First you subtract the number of wins the trailer has from the number of wins the leader has. In the example above, the Toronto Blue Jays are the leaders in the American League East, with 12 wins. If you want to see how far behind the Blue Jays the Baltimore Orioles are, you subtract the Orioles' wins (8) from the Blue Jays' wins (12), for a total of 4.

Next you subtract the leader's losses (3) from the trailer's losses (5), for a total of 2. You then add the two numbers you have just computed and find their average by dividing this number by two. In this case, the average of 4 and 2 is 3. This is the games behind number. In other words, the Baltimore Orioles are 3 games behind the first-place leaders, the Toronto Blue Jays. If a team has a GB of zero, that means it is tied for first place. This is usually shown by a -- in the GB column. If two teams are tied for first place, then you have to see who has the better winning percentage to determine who is actually ahead.

As the season winds down, especially in baseball, you will find that newspapers and broadcasters talk a lot about the first-place team's **magic number.** This is the combination of wins by the first-place team and losses by its closest competitors. As the teams competing for first place win and lose, the magic number shrinks. Eventually, when it becomes zero, someone has won the division title.

To find a team's magic number, first take the total number of scheduled games in a sport's season (162 in baseball, 82 in basketball, 16 in football) and add one. Next, add the first-place team's number of wins to the number of losses of the team you are comparing it to. Finally, subtract the second number from the first number.

The result is the magic number for the first-place team. The lower the magic number is, the less likely it is that the team trailing the leader in the standings will catch up. If the magic number is one, the best that the trailer can do is tie the leader. If the number is zero or less, the trailer can no longer win the division. If all the teams below the leader have a magic number of zero or less, then the leader has clinched, or won, the top spot in the division.

Look at the diagram below, listing standings in the National Basketball Association (NBA). In the Atlantic Division of the Eastern Conference, the New York Knicks

NBA STANDINGS
Atlantic

	W	L	Pct.	GB	Last 10	Home	Away	Conf.
Knicks	48	29	.623	—	6–4	28–11	20–18	31–20
Boston	46	31	.597	2	9–1	32– 7	14–24	30–21
Nets	36	40	.474	11½	6–4	23–15	13–25	25–25
Miami	35	42	.455	13	5–5	26–12	9–30	24–27
Philidelphia	33	43	.434	14½	3–7	22–16	11–27	21–29
Washington	24	53	.312	24	2–8	13–26	11–27	14–37
Orlando	19	57	.250	28½	4–6	11–27	8–30	14–37

are the leaders, with 48 wins. The Boston Celtics are second, with 46 wins. To find the Knicks' magic number, you take the total number of games in the basketball season (82) and add one, for a total of 83. You then add the leader's wins (48) to the trailer's losses (31), for a total of 79. Subtracting 79 from 83, you find that the Knicks' magic number is 4. If the Knicks win their next two games and Boston wins one and loses one, the Knicks' magic number will drop to one, and the best that Boston can do is tie for first place.

Since football and basketball allow more than just the division winner to go to the playoffs, the magic number isn't as important as it is in baseball, where only the team that finishes in first place gets a spot in the playoffs. The magic number does, however, tell us how hard or easy it is for the leader to hold on to first place.

When you look at the box that lists the league standings, you may see several other columns with numbers. People aren't only interested in a team's total record of wins and losses. They also want to know how teams perform under different conditions. You might see a column labeled **Last 10**. This column contains information on how a team performed in its last 10 games. In the NBA standings on the previous page, this column shows that, over the last 10 games played, the Knicks won 6 and lost 4. There might also be columns showing how a team performed at home and away. In the case of the Knicks, we see that they won 28 home games and lost 11. In away games, they have won 20 and lost 18.

In baseball there may even be columns that show how teams have performed on artificial turf compared to grass fields or in night games compared to day games.

Now that you know some statistics common to all sports, we'll take a more detailed look at the types of numbers used to give us information about the Big Three sports: baseball, basketball, and football.

1. BASEBALL

*O*f all the sports found on the sports pages, baseball has the most statistics. There are far too many baseball stats to be discussed in any one book. In fact, there are several baseball encyclopedias with thousands of pages of statistics, and even these don't include all the stats there are. The information tables for baseball are crammed with numbers, and newspapers are constantly coming up with new ones.

There is even a group of baseball enthusiasts called the Society for American Baseball Research (SABR) that has started a form of statistical study called **sabermetrics,** which searches for the perfect baseball statistic. While sabermetrics hasn't found that elusive statistic yet, it, too, is coming up with new ways to analyze players' and teams' abilities.

Despite all these different and ever-changing stats, there are certain basic stats that will always be on baseball cards, appear on sports pages, and be used by sportscasters. These are the ones we will concentrate on.

STANDINGS

Baseball standings are just like the ones you read about in the introduction. Baseball teams are ranked according to their wins and losses, their winning percentage, and the number of games behind the leader they are. Professional baseball teams are divided into two leagues, the American League and the National League. In addition, each league is divided into two divisions, the East and the West. This is done because it helps to organize the many different teams and helps in setting up a schedule of games for the season.

There are also different rules for the teams in different leagues. In the National League, for example, pitchers must take a turn at bat just like the other players. If a team's manager wants to put in a batter who hits better than his pitcher, he must remove his pitcher from the game. In the American League, however, the manager can select a batter, called a **designated hitter,** to take the pitcher's turn at bat. This allows a batter who might not be a good fielder to do what he is good at, batting, while the pitcher he is replacing takes his place in the field.

BOX SCORES

In baseball there are three main kinds of statistics: **pitching statistics, batting statistics** (also called **offensive statistics),** and **fielding statistics** (also called **defensive statistics**). In the National League, pitchers have all three types of statistics, while in the American League pitchers do not bat and therefore have only fielding and pitching statistics.

The basic chart used to give statistics for individual baseball games (and individual games in all other sports) is the **box score.** Baseball box scores will normally look like the one in the diagram on page 21. Some papers may add different stats to this basic box score, but for the most part you will always see the players listed in the order in which they batted in the game, with the stats in columns next to their names. Next to each player's name there may be a code that shows what position he started the game in. In the example on the next page, for a game between the Atlanta Braves and the New York Mets, we see that Nixon of the Atlanta Braves was the first batter for the Braves and he started the game playing left field (lf).

Braves 8
Mets 6

ATLANTA	ab	r	h	bi	METS	ab	r	h	bi
Nixon lf	5	1	2	1	Coleman lf	3	0	0	0
Sanders cf	3	1	2	1	Gibson p	0	0	0	0
Moore cf	2	0	0	0	McCry ph	1	0	0	0
Pendltn 3b	3	2	0	0	Franco p	0	0	0	0
Rodrigz 3b	1	1	1	2	Burke p	0	0	0	0
Bream 1b	2	0	0	0	Sasser ph	1	0	0	0
Cabrer 1b	2	0	0	0	Rndlph 2b	2	1	1	0
Hunter rf	3	1	1	1	Noboa 2b	2	0	1	1
Rivera p	0	0	0	0	Bonilla rf	3	0	1	0
Willard ph	1	0	0	0	Gallghr rf	2	1	1	1
Berengr p	0	0	0	0	Johnson cf	4	2	3	1
Berryhill c	3	1	0	0	Murray 1b	3	0	0	0
Lyons 2b	2	0	0	1	McKng 1b	1	0	1	1
Belliard ss	3	1	2	2	Pecota 3b	5	0	3	0
Castilla ss	1	0	0	0	Elster ss	4	0	0	0
Bielecki p	1	0	0	0	O'Brien c	4	1	1	0
Carabal 2b	1	0	0	0	Cone p	1	0	0	0
					Innis p	0	0	0	0
					Boston lf	3	1	1	1
Totals	**33**	**8**	**8**	**8**	**Totals**	**39**	**6**	**13**	**5**

Atlanta	003	030	002—8
New York	001	000	113—6

E—Murray 2, Bonilla, Lyons, Rodriguez, Berryhill. DP—Atlanta 1. LOB—Atlanta 6, New York 9. 2B—Belliard, Hunter, Johnson. HR—Sanders (1), Rodriguez (1), Boston (2), Gallagher (1). SB—Pecota (4), Sanders 2 (11), Johnson (4), Nixon (9), McKnight (1). CS—Nixon, Sanders. S—Bielecki.

	IP	H	R	ER	BB	SO
Atlanta						
Bielecki W, 1-1	6	5	1	1	2	8
Rivera	2	5	2	1	0	2
Berenguer	1	3	3	2	1	1
New York						
Cone L, 1-3	4 ⅔	5	6	5	7	6
Innis	⅓	1	0	0	0	0
Gibson	2	0	0	0	0	0
Franco	1	0	0	0	0	2
Burke	1	2	2	2	0	1

T—3:08. A—6,579.

BATTING STATISTICS

The four columns after a player's name show the four most important batting statistics: **at-bats, runs, hits,** and **runs batted in.** These stats are designated **AB, R, H,** and **BI** or **RBI.**

In the box score on page 21, we see that Howard Johnson of the Mets played center field in the game against Atlanta, had 4 at-bats, scored 2 runs, had 3 hits, and had one run batted in.

At the bottom of each team's listing, the totals for the four columns are added up. The Atlanta Braves, for instance, went to bat 33 times, got 8 runs off of 8 hits, and had 8 runs batted in.

What do all these statistics mean? An at-bat is any time a player goes to bat and does anything other than get a walk, get hit by a pitch, lay down a **sacrifice bunt** (a little hit into the infield that allows runners on base to advance but results in the batter being thrown out), or hit a **sacrifice fly** (a fly ball hit to the outfield that, while caught, allows a runner on third base to get home and score a run). Because of these exceptions, it is possible that a player could reach home plate once or even a number of times and never be given an official at-bat. Although it does not appear in the box score, we say that every time a batter comes to the plate, regardless of what he does, he is given a **plate appearance.**

A run is credited to a player when he crosses home plate as a baserunner and scores a point, or run, for his team. A hit is given to a player who puts the ball into play and reaches a base safely as a result of anything other than a fielding error by the other team or by forcing another runner out. Players who reach base safely because of a misplayed ball are said to have reached base on a fielding error and are not credited with a hit. Home runs are considered hits. A hit may also be credited to a player who successfully reaches first base but is tagged out when he tries to reach second. If Boston's third baseman, Wade Boggs, reaches first base on a hit, for example, but is tagged out while trying to reach second, he is given credit for a hit—a single—even though his team makes an out as well.

Runs batted in are given to players who, through their hitting, move either themselves or another player to home plate to score a run. If a player gets a base hit that allows another player to score, he is credited with one RBI. If he hits a home run, he gets one RBI for himself, plus one for each of the other players that his home run allows to reach home plate. Even if the batter is called out, he is credited with an RBI if someone else scores off of his trip to the plate.

There is one exception to this rule: If a batter hits into a **double play,** a play in which the batter plus one additional baserunner is called out because of good defensive play, the batter does not get an RBI, even if a third runner manages to score.

This is a lot to remember, so don't feel bad if you forget some of it. If it makes you feel any better, baseball rules are so complicated that there is a person called the **official scorer** at every game whose job it is to figure out what is considered a hit, what's an error, and who gets credited with RBIs.

SCORING SUMMARIES

Following a team's batting statistics, there will be a listing that shows when the teams scored their runs. This is called a **scoring summary.** The visiting team will appear first, followed by a number for each **inning** played in the game. There are normally 9 innings, but rain or overtime can result in fewer or extra innings. Each number shows the number of runs a team got in a particular inning, with a final number at the end showing the total number of runs. The same process is repeated on the line below, for the home team. In baseball, a home team does not have to bat in the last inning of a game in which it is leading. If the team did not bat, there will be an X for the last inning of the game.

If you look back at our original box score, you can see the scoring summary for the game between Atlanta and New York. The visiting team, Atlanta, scored no runs in the first 2 innings, 3 runs in the third inning, no runs in the fourth, 3 in the fifth, none in the sixth, seventh, or eighth, and 2 more in the ninth, for a total of 8 runs. New York, the home team, scored no runs in the first or second innings, one in the third, none in the fourth, fifth, or sixth innings, one each in the seventh and eighth, and 3 in the ninth, for a total of 6.

FIELDING AND OTHER STATISTICS

After the scoring summary, you will find some other team and individual statistics, with a listing of who did what and how many times. Players who committed **errors—** defensive mistakes such as dropping a ball or making a bad throw that allows a runner to reach base safely—are listed first. In our example, we see that Murray of the Mets had 2 errors, while Bonilla, Lyons, Rodriguez, and Berryhill each had one.

After the errors are the **double plays,** or **DPs.** These are defensive plays in which two baserunners are called out on one good play. In our game, Atlanta had one double play.

The next statistic is for players **left on base,** or **LOB.** These are players who reach base but do not score a run because their team gets 3 outs before they have a chance to reach home. From our box score, we see that the Braves had 6 players LOB while the Mets had 9. Getting left on base is a mixed bag, because having players LOB means that a team got runners on base but, unfortunately, couldn't get any RBIs to let them score.

Following the LOBs is a listing of **extra-base hits.** An extra-base hit is any hit other than a single. This includes doubles, triples, and home runs. Each of these types of hits is listed individually, starting with doubles. The players who made these hits are listed by name. Some box scores also have numbers in parentheses that show how many of a particular type of hit the player has made in an entire season. Belliard and Hunter of Atlanta both hit doubles in the game against the Mets, while Johnson of New York hit one. Sanders, Rodriguez, and Gallagher each hit their first homers, and Boston had his second of the season.

The last kind of information found in this part of the box score has to do with players who steal bases (SB), get caught while trying to steal bases (CS), lay down sacrifices (S), and hit sacrifice flies (SF). As before, the player's name is listed, followed by a number showing his total for the season in that particular stat. There were 6 stolen bases in our example, with the most going to Sanders of Atlanta, who took 2, for a season total of 11. Two Atlanta players, Nixon and Sanders, were caught stealing, and one, Bielecki of the Braves, hit a sacrifice bunt.

PITCHING STATISTICS

At the bottom of the box score are all the pitching statistics for the game. Pitching statistics are also listed in rows and columns, just like batting stats. While batters have only 4 columns of stats, pitchers have 6. They are **innings pitched, hits allowed, runs allowed, earned runs allowed, walks allowed,** and **strikeouts.** These are designated **IP, H, R, ER, BB,** and **SO.**

A pitcher is given an inning pitched for every 3 outs he

gets while pitching. Pitchers can also be given fractions of an inning pitched. Each out counts as one-third of an inning, so if a pitcher gets 4 batters out, he is said to have pitched one and a third innings. In the box score above, Cone of New York is credited with 4⅔ innings pitched. This means that he got out 14 batters.

Hits allowed are the number of hits the pitcher allows while he is pitching in the game. Cone, the losing pitcher in our example, allowed five hits during his 4⅔ innings on the mound. Bielecki, the winning pitcher, also gave up five hits.

Runs allowed are the number of baserunners that the pitcher allowed to cross home plate to score a run. How the runners get to home plate does not matter. They can hit a home run, score on another player's hit, or reach home on an error. Even if a pitcher is removed from a game in the middle of an inning, if a runner who reached base while he was pitching then scored, the removed pitcher is said to have given up the run. In the game against the Braves, Cone allowed 6 runners to score. Bielecki, on the other hand, allowed only one batter to reach home plate during his 6 innings pitched.

Earned runs are a little more complicated. In general, when the fielders behind the pitcher make errors, we say that the runs are not the pitcher's fault and are therefore unearned. For example, when a batter who reaches base because of an error scores a run, when a run is batted in because of an error (and no RBI is given to the batter), or when a fielding error prevents what would have been the third and final out of an inning, the resulting run is unearned. Any runs that are scored without the help of fielding errors are considered earned runs.

A walk is labeled BB, which stands for a base on balls. A walk is awarded to a batter when the pitcher throws 4 pitches that are out of the batter's **strike zone** and the batter does not swing at them. These out-of-range pitches are called balls. If a pitcher throws 4 balls, the batter goes to first base without having to hit a pitch. If the batter does swing at a pitch that is out of his strike zone and misses, then it is counted as a strike rather than a ball. This stat shows how many times a pitcher lets a player get to first base because he threw balls.

The final column, strikeouts, shows how many times a pitcher threw 3 pitches that a batter either swung at and missed, fouled out on, or else were in the batter's strike zone but were not swung at.

In addition to the columns of stats, there may be some letters and numbers next to the names of the pitchers who played in the game. The pitcher who won the game will have a **W** next to his name, along with his new won-loss record. The pitcher who lost will have an **L,** together with his new won-loss record. A pitcher who got a **save** will have an **S** by his name and the number of saves he has earned during the season.

To be considered the winning pitcher, a pitcher must have pitched 5 innings from the start of the game and left the game with the lead, or else come into the game with the score tied or while his team is losing and pitch well enough so that his team takes the lead and goes on to win.

A losing pitcher is the one who gives up the winning run to the other team. To be credited with a save, a pitcher must come into a game while his team has the lead and hold that lead. He must either pitch 3 innings, or hold his team's lead when the other team has one or more runners on base and has the potential to tie the game or take the lead if the next batter up scores a run.

MISCELLANEOUS STATISTICS

After all the pitching statistics are listed, there is sometimes a set of listings at the bottom of the box score for miscellaneous information. This can include batters who have been hit by pitches and allowed to walk to first base (along with the names of the pitchers who hit them), pitchers who **balked** (violated a rule about pitching motion) or threw **wild pitches** (pitches that get past the catcher because of the pitcher's error and allow a runner to advance a base), and catchers who gave up **passed balls** (pitches that get past the catcher because of his error and allow a runner to advance a base). At the very end, newspapers sometimes list the names of the umpires who officiated the game, the total length of time the game took to play, and the attendance at the game. In our example, the game between New York and Atlanta took 3 hours and 8 minutes, and the total number of paid attendance was 6,579.

LINE SCORES

For most college baseball games, and for professional games that are held during the spring-training season, newspapers don't always print the results of games in a box score. In that case, you might see a second type of diagram called a **line score.** A line score doesn't tell us as much about a game as a box score does, but it tells us enough to give a good idea of what happened. Line scores first list the teams and their scores by innings, just as a box score does. The line score on the next page shows the results of a game between the Minnesota Twins and the Baltimore Orioles. Baltimore was the losing team, with 5 runs. Minnesota, the home team, had 6. Notice that Minnesota has an **X** in the ninth inning to indicate that they did not have to bat because they were ahead.

After the runs are listed by innings, a line score has a pitching summary, with all the pitchers listed by team in the order that they appeared. Pitchers other than the starter have a number in parentheses next to their names, indicating the inning in which they started. After all the pitchers are listed is the name of the catcher who caught for the team during the game.

In this particular game, Mussina was the starting pitcher for Baltimore. He was replaced in the seventh inning by Rasmussen. Hoiles was the starting catcher, and he was replaced in the seventh inning by Parent. For Minnesota, Tapani started the game and was replaced on the pitching mound by Banks in the sixth inning. Harper was the catcher for the Twins, with Parks coming in to play the last inning.

The winning pitcher, losing pitcher, and saving pitcher are listed next, with their updated records. Banks, the winning pitcher for Minnesota, is now credited with 2 wins and no losses. The losing pitcher, Rasmussen, has a record of one win and one loss as a result of the game.

After the pitching information, there will be a listing for all the home runs scored during the game. Players hitting home runs will be listed by name, with their season home-run total in parentheses. In this game, 2 Orioles, Hoiles and Martinez, hit homers giving them new totals of 4 and 2, respectively. One Twins player, Quinones, hit a home run, for a season total of 4.

After all the stats, you might also find a very short

batting average for the 1991 season, first find the number of hits he had. This is in the column labeled H. Looking in this column, you see that Sax had 198 hits in 1991. By looking in the at-bat, or AB column, you see that he went to bat 652 times. By dividing 652 into 198, you get Sax's batting average: .304.

The batting average gives you a general idea of how well a player hits. Any batting average over .270 is good,

STEVE SAX

Height: 6'0"   Weight: 182

Bats: Right   Throws: Right

Born 1-29-60   W. Sacramento, CA

Home: Manhattan Beach, CA

Yr.	Club	Pct.	G	AB	R	H	2B	3B	HR	RBI	SB	BB	SO
78	Lethbrge	.328	39	131	24	43	6	3	0	21	0	16	20
79	Clinton	.290	115	386	64	112	15	2	2	52	25	57	30
80	Vero Bch	.283	139	530	78	150	18	8	3	61	33	51	26
81	SanAnton	.346	115	485	94	168	23	3	8	52	34	40	32
81	Dodgers	.277	31	119	15	33	2	0	2	9	5	7	14
82	Dodgers	.282	150	638	88	180	23	7	4	47	49	49	53
83	Dodgers	.281	155	623	94	175	18	5	5	41	56	58	73
84	Dodgers	.243	145	569	70	138	24	4	1	35	34	47	53
85	Dodgers	.279	136	488	62	136	8	4	1	42	27	54	43
86	Dodgers	.332	157	633	91	210	43	4	6	56	40	59	58
87	Dodgers	.280	157	610	84	171	22	7	6	46	37	44	61
88	Dodgers	.277	160	632	70	175	19	4	5	57	42	45	51
89	Yankees	.315	158	651	88	205	26	3	5	63	43	52	44
90	Yankees	.260	155	615	70	160	24	2	4	42	43	49	46
91	Yankees	.304	158	652	85	198	38	2	10	56	31	41	38
ML	Totals	.286	1562	6230	817	1781	247	42	49	494	407	505	534

anything over .300 is great, and anything higher than .330 or so is tremendous. Players very rarely bat over .400 over the course of a season. The last batter to accomplish this feat was Boston's Ted Williams, who hit .406 in 1941.

Batting average isn't the only important stat. It doesn't tell anything about what type of hits a player hits most often. Nor does it show how many times a player was walked. The number of walks a player receives is important because it says something about how carefully he chooses the pitches he swings at. A hitter who walks 90 times and has a batting average of .250 may, in fact, be a more valuable player than one who walks only 10 times but has a higher batting average of .310. A player who gets walked often is one who watches pitches closely and swings only at those he thinks are in his strike range. A player who walks infrequently is one who swings at most of the pitches thrown at him.

Similarly, a batter who hits 30 home runs, 20 doubles, and 10 triples while batting .300 is certainly more valuable than another .330 hitter with only 2 home runs, 10 doubles, and 5 triples. To help even things out, statistics called **on-base percentage** (OB%) and **slugging percentage** (SL%, or SLG) have been created. On-base percentage is the number of hits and walks a player has, plus the number of times he was hit by a pitch, divided by his number of plate appearances. (A **hit-by-pitch** is when a player is actually hit by a pitched ball and is allowed to go to first base.) An OB% of .350 or better is considered good, while numbers over .400 are outstanding. On-base percentage is a more telling stat than batting average because it shows how often a player is likely to reach base.

Slugging percentage helps measure the types of hits a player will get. While singles, doubles, triples, and home runs are all considered hits, a hit that gets a player around 4 bases is better than one that gets him only to

HT: 6'3" WT: 225 BATS: RIGHT THROWS: RIGHT
DRAFT: GIANTS #4-JUNE, 1978
ACQ: FREE AGENT, 11-21-90 BORN: 9-29-60, ORANGE, CALIFORNIA
HOME: GILBERT, ARIZONA

COMPLETE MAJOR LEAGUE BATTING RECORD (LEAGUE LEADER IN ITALICS, TIE•)

YR CLUB	G	AB	R	H	2B	3B	HR	RBI	SB	SLG	BB	SO	AVG
84 GIANTS	13	24	5	4	0	0	3	3	1	.542	7	10	.167
85 GIANTS	78	162	22	30	5	1	8	20	0	.377	23	71	.185
86 BREWERS	134	466	75	108	17	3	33	86	5	.494	72	179	.232
87 BREWERS	134	474	71	113	15	2	28	80	12	.456	86	186	.238
88 BREWERS	135	492	71	124	24	0	23	85	9	.441	51	153•	.252
89 BREWERS	130	466	72	98	18	2	26	65	4	.425	60	158	.210
90 BREWERS	134	440	57	92	15	1	27	69	2	.432	64	147	.209
91 TIGERS	134	448	64	80	14	2	25	64	1	.386	89	175	.179
MAJ. LEA. TLS.	**892**	**2972**	**437**	**649**	**108**	**11**	**173**	**472**	**34**	**.437**	**452**	**1079**	**.218**

one. Slugging percentage was created to reflect whether a player most often hits singles, doubles, triples, or home runs. To compute slugging percentage, we start with a stat called **total bases.** To find total bases, you add up the number of bases a player has reached. A single is worth one base, a double is worth 2, a triple 3, and a home run 4.

Look at the baseball card for outfielder Rob Deer of the Detroit Tigers. During the 1991 season, Deer hit 25 home runs, 2 triples, 14 doubles, and 39 singles, for a total of 173 bases. (To find the number of singles, add up home runs, triples, and doubles and subtract that from the total number of hits shown in the H column.) Divided by Deer's total at-bats, 448, we get a slugging percentage of .386.

Because home runs, triples, and doubles are all worth more than one point, it is possible to have a slugging percentage greater than 1.000. A player who hits a home run every time he comes to the plate would have a slugging percentage of 4.000. That has never happened, though, except when a player has batted only once or twice in a season. A good SL% is around .450, an excellent one is over .500, and the best players ever have been well above .600.

Pitching statistics that you might find on a baseball card are similar to the ones found in a newspaper's box score. Among other things, you will find a pitcher's won-loss record, the number of games he has pitched in, the number of innings he has pitched, and his strikeout totals.

The sample baseball card below contains information about pitcher Mike Bielecki, of the Atlanta Braves. By looking in the appropriate columns, we see that, while playing for the Chicago Cubs in 1991, Bielecki had 13 wins (W) and 11 losses (L). In 39 games (G), he pitched for 172 innings (IP) and had 72 strikeouts (SO).

Another pitching stat that is of great interest to baseball fans is **earned run average.** Earned run average (ERA) measures how many earned runs a pitcher can be expected to give up in a 9-inning, or complete, game. Remember that an earned run is any run that is the pitcher's fault and not caused by fielding errors or passed balls. To find a pitcher's ERA, divide the number of earned runs he gave up (usually found in a column

---

MIKE BIELECKI P   **26**

HT: 6'3" WT: 195 BATS: RIGHT THROWS: RIGHT
DRFT: PIRATES #1(PEC)-JUNE, 1979
ACQ: TRADE, 9-29-91 BORN: 7-31-59, BALTIMORE, MARYLAND
HOME: CHICAGO, ILL.
COMPLETE MAJOR LEAGUE PITCHING RECORD

YR	CLUB	G	IP	W	L	R	ER	SO	BB	GS	CG	SHO	SV	ERA
84	PIRATES	4	4.1	0	0	0	0	1	0	0	0	0	0	0.00
85	PIRATES	12	45.2	2	3	26	23	22	31	7	0	0	0	4.53
86	PIRATES	31	148.2	6	11	87	77	83	83	27	0	0	0	4.66
87	PIRATES	8	45.2	2	3	25	24	25	12	8	2	0	0	4.73
88	CUBS	19	48.1	2	2	22	18	33	16	5	0	0	0	3.35
89	CUBS	33	212.1	18	7	82	74	147	81	33	4	3	0	3.14
90	CUBS	36	168	8	11	101	92	103	70	29	0	0	1	4.93
91	CUBS	39	172	13	11	91	86	72	54	25	0	0	0	4.5
91	BRAVES	2	1.2	0	0	0	0	3	2	0	0	0	0	0.00
MAJ. LEA. TLS		184	846.2	51	48	434	394	489	349	134	6	3	1	4.19

labeled **ER**) by the total number of innings pitched, including thirds of innings. Multiply the result by 9, and you have a pitcher's ERA. In Mike Bielecki's case, in 1991 he gave up 86 runs in 172 innings. If we divide 86 by 172 and multiply the result by 9, we get 4.50, Bielecki's ERA for the 1991 season with the Cubs.

Another stat that is given as part of a player's season statistics is **complete games, or CG.** Complete games are given to pitchers who pitch an entire game for their team, usually 8 or 9 innings in a normal game. If a game goes to extra innings, the pitcher would still have to pitch in these extra innings to be given a complete game. Regardless of the length of a complete game, if a pitcher does not allow any runs during the game, he is credited with a **shutout, or SHO.** From reading Mike Bielecki's card, we can see that he has not pitched any complete games or had any shutouts since 1989. In that year he pitched 4 complete games, 3 of them shutouts.

The two most coveted pitching statistics are **no-hitters** and **perfect games.** These two pitching feats get a tremendous amount of attention from reporters, broadcasters, and fans. A pitcher is credited with a no-hitter if he doesn't allow the other team to get any base hits during an entire nine-inning game. Strangely enough, a pitcher can sometimes lose a game while throwing a no-hitter. Former New York Yankee Andy Hawkins lost a no-hitter 4–0 when his team made several fielding errors late in the game.

Pitchers are said to have pitched a perfect game if they do not allow any batters to reach base in any way over a complete game. There can be no hits, no errors, no walks, and no hit-by-pitches. Perfect games are also, by definition, no-hitters. There is no way a pitcher can receive credit for a perfect game and lose.

THE GREAT DEBATE

Statistics are often used to resolve debates among fans about the greatest players and performances of all time. In baseball, one such debate is about which player has hit the most home runs in a season. In 1927, George Herman "Babe" Ruth hit 60 home runs for the New York Yankees. But 34 years later, another Yankee, Roger Maris, hit 61. One would think that Maris is obviously the player who hit the most home runs in a season.

But a debate rages over how many games and at-bats it took for each player to reach his final total. Ruth hit his 60 homers in 151 games and 540 at-bats. Maris, on the other hand, needed 161 games and 590 at-bats to reach his total. When Ruth played, teams only played 154 games during a season, while now they play 162.

Maris would seem to have an unfair advantage over Ruth. As a result, statisticians have looked at Ruth's per-game and per-at-bat home run averages and estimated what he would have hit if he had actually been able to play in 161 games, as Maris did. To do this, they first divided the number of games Ruth played by his total number of home runs and found that he hit a homer every 2.5 games. If Ruth had been able to play the extra 10 games that Maris played, he would have been expected to hit another 4 home runs, for a total of 64, 3 more than Maris hit in the same number of games.

We can do the same thing using at-bats. Dividing Ruth's at-bats by his homers, we find that he hit a home run every 9 at-bats. If he had the extra 50 at-bats that Maris had, we would expect him to have hit about 5 more homers, again beating Maris's record.

As you can see, stats can be used to argue for different interpretations of sports records. Maris is officially credited with the most home runs during a season, but many argue that Ruth still deserves the honor. You can also see from what we just did that it is very easy to create sports statistics. You should now be able to create some statistics of your own.

But don't think that baseball stats are all there is. In the next two chapters, you will learn about basketball and football, two games that are followed just as closely as baseball and that have stats that are just as much fun to learn about.

2. BASKETBALL

*B*asketball, which has just celebrated its 100th anniversary, has grown to be one of the most popular games in the world. Professional leagues have been formed on several continents and in many countries. In the United States, fans follow both professional and college basketball with equal enthusiasm. In some states, even high-school basketball is very popular.

The National Basketball Association (NBA) is divided into two conferences, with two divisions in each conference. There is an Eastern Conference, made up of teams from the eastern part of the United States, and Western Conference, consisting of teams in the western part of the United States. The Eastern Conference has an Atlantic Division, made up of teams on the Atlantic Coast, like the New York Knicks and New Jersey Nets, and a Central Division, comprised of teams that are not on the coast, like the Indiana Pacers and Chicago Bulls. The Western Conference has a Midwest Division, home to teams such as the San Antonio Spurs, Houston Rockets, and Denver Nuggets, and a Pacific Division, made up of teams on the Pacific Coast, such as the Los Angeles Lakers and Seattle Supersonics.

STANDINGS

As in baseball, overall standings in basketball are based on wins and losses. For an example of a basketball standings chart, look in the section on standings in the introduction.

BOX SCORES: THE SHORT FORM

There are two kinds of basketball box scores that you will find in a newspaper. The first type of box score is called the **short form.** Most college basketball games will appear in this kind of form, and occasionally pro games do as well. A diagram of a short form appears below.

In a short form, the visiting team appears first, with the total number of points scored in parentheses. In the diagram below, Columbia played at Cornell and scored 85 points to Cornell's 70.

A listing of each team's players is then given. Listed after each player's name is a set of five numbers. These numbers represent **field goals** made (shots worth either 2 or 3 points), field goals attempted, **free throws** made (foul shots worth one point apiece), free throws attempted, and total points scored. In the listing for Columbia, Steward made 6 field goals in 15 attempts. He also took 2

Columbia (85)
Steward 6-15 2-2 17, Downing 4-7 2-2 11, Casey 6-7 7-10 19, Sanders 1-2 0-0 2, Jenkins 11-18 8-10 32, Speaker 0-2 2, Dumolien 1-2 0-0 2, Holmes 1-2 0-0 2, Brady 0-0 0-0 0, Waterer 0-0 0-0 0, Buckelew 0-0 0-0 0

Cornell (70)
Medina 7-14 3-4 17, Marshall 7-12 1-3 15, Treadwell 3-6 0-0 6, Gaca 7-22 0-0 21, Maharaj 2-11 4-4 9, Parker 0-0 0-0 0, Kopf 0-2 0-0 0, Thwaites 1-1 0-0 2, Hayes 0-0 0-0 0

Halftime–Columbia 36, Cornell 29. 3-point goals–Columbia 6-8 (Steward 3-4, Jenkins 2-2, Downing 1-2), Cornell 8-20 (Gaca 7-12, Maharaj 1-8). Fouled Out– Marshall. Rebounds–Columbia 43 (Downing-11), Cornell 29 (Medina-8). Assists–Columbia 8 (Downing 3), Cornell 11 (Maharaj 4). Total Fouls–Columbia 11, Cornell 22. A–4,000.

---

free throws, and made both of them. Steward scored 17 points for Columbia in the entire game. After all of the players have been listed, the team totals may also be listed in the same manner.

After both teams have been listed, there is a listing for other important team statistics from the game. For a college game, a halftime score is given, because college games are made up of two 20-minute halves. For a pro game, which consists of four 12-minute quarters, a score by quarters is given. At halftime, Columbia was leading Cornell 36 to 29.

After the halftime or quarter scores are numbers for **3-point goals** made and attempted. A 3-point shot is one that is made from a certain distance away from the basket. In a short form, the total 3-point shot stats are given for a team, followed by stats for individual players. In the Columbia-Cornell game, Cornell made 8 out of 20 attempted 3-point shots. Seven of these were made by Gaca, who attempted 12, and one was made by Maharaj, who attempted 8. A player's 3-point shots are included in his overall shot attempts mentioned earlier.

After the 3-pointer listing is a stat that players try to avoid: fouling out. Players whose names appear here are ones who were charged with either 5 (in a college game) or 6 (in a pro game) fouls and were required to sit out the remainder of the game. One player, Marshall of Cornell, fouled out during the game.

Rebounds and **assists** are listed next. A rebound is a missed shot that a player gains control of by grabbing the ball as it bounces off the backboard or rim of the basket. An assist is a pass that directly sets up another player for a basket. In a short form, the total number of rebounds and assists are given for each team, followed by the name of the player who led the team in each category and the number the player made. Columbia had 43 rebounds, 11 of them made by Downing. Cornell had 11 assists, led by Maharaj's 4.

Finally, the total number of fouls made by each team is listed, and the number of people who attended the game may also be given.

BOX SCORES: THE LONG FORM

The **long form** of the box score is more complicated, but it gives a better understanding of what each individual player did during a game. Generally, it is used more for professional games than for college games.

As with the short form box score, the visiting team is listed first. Players are listed in the first column, followed by different statistics. The first column, **M**, lists the number of minutes the player played during the game. There are 48 minutes in a standard pro basketball game that does not go into overtime.

Listed after the minutes played are field goals (**FG**) attempted, then free throws (**FT**) made and attempted, just as in the short form.

The next column is labeled **O-R**. This column gives information about the rebounds a player made. The first number listed is the number of **offensive rebounds** the player made. An offensive rebound is a rebound that is made after a player's own team missed a shot at the basket. The second number is the total number of rebounds, both offensive and defensive, a player made. If you subtract the offensive rebounds from the total rebounds, you get the number of **defensive rebounds** made by the player. A defensive rebound is one made from an opponent's missed shot.

After rebounds are listed, there is a column labeled **A** for assists and one labeled **PF** for personal fouls, the number of fouls a player committed. Finally there is a column for total points, or **PTS**. This tells how many points a player scored during a game.

On page 43 is a long form for a game between the

Celtics 93, Knicks 89

KNICKS

	m	fg	ft	o-r	a	pf	pts
McDaniel	16	3-5	3-4	1-3	1	2	9
Oakley	24	0-4	0-0	1-6	0	3	0
Ewing	42	13-26	8-8	4-10	1	2	35
Jackson	33	2-9	3-4	0-1	9	2	7
Wilkins	21	2-8	0-0	0-2	1	2	4
Starks	36	7-14	1-1	0-4	5	6	16
Mason	35	4-8	2-2	2-8	1	0	10
Vandwghe	18	2-7	2-2	0-1	1	1	6
Anthony	15	1-3	0-0	0-0	3	3	2
Totals	240	34-84	19-21	8-35	22	21	89

Three-point goals: 2-11, .182 (Ewing 1-2, Starks 1-5, Jackson 0-1, Vandeweghe 0-1, Wilkins 0-2). **Team rebounds:** 14. **Blocked shots:** 5 (Ewing 3, Mason, Anthony). **Turnovers:** 14 (Ewing 3, Jackson 3, Wilkins 3, Starks 2, Oakley, Vandeweghe, Anthony). **Steals:** 8 (Ewing 2, Jackson 2, Starks 2, McDaniel, Vandeweghe). **Technicals:** Ewing, 3:56 4th.

	m	fg	ft	o-r	a	pf	pts
Gamble	38	6-15	1-1	1-3	5	1	13
Pinckney	22	3-3	0-0	3-8	2	1	6
Parish	37	7-15	0-0	1-11	0	5	14
Brown	22	3-3	1-2	1-3	3	1	8
Lewis	41	5-12	5-7	0-6	4	3	15
McHale	25	6-13	3-6	3-5	0	1	15
Bagley	26	6-12	0-2	0-1	5	0	13
Kleine	10	2-4	0-0	0-3	0	4	4
Fox	19	2-2	0-0	0-1	5	2	5
Totals	240	40-79	10-18	9-41	24	18	93

Three-point goals: 3-4, .750 (Brown 1-1, Bagley 1-1, Fox 1-1, Gamble 0-1). **Team rebounds:** 9. **Blocked shots:** 7 (Gamble 2, Parish 2, Lewis 2, Fox). **Turnovers:** 14 (Brown 4, McHale 4, Pinckney 2, Parish 2, Gamble, Lewis). **Steals:** 10 (Parish 3, Bagley 3, Gamble, Pinckney, Lewis, Fox).

KNICKS		22 23 20 24—89
BOSTON		23 30 18 22—93

A: 14,890 **T:** 2:06. **Officials:** Ed T. Rush, Jim Kinsey, Greg Willard.

Boston Celtics and the New York Knicks. Let's look at the stats for Patrick Ewing of the Knicks. Using what we know about the long form, we see that Ewing played for 42 of the game's 48 minutes. During that time, he made 13 out of 26 attempted field goals and 8 of 8 free throws. Ewing also had a total of 10 rebounds. Since 4 of them were offensive, we can subtract that from his total and find that 6 were defensive rebounds. Finally we see that he had one assist, 2 personal fouls, and scored a total of 35 points for the Knicks.

Below the individual stat listings for the team you will find a listing of team percentages. There are percentages for field goal shooting, 3-point shooting, and foul shooting. To find a percentage for any of these three types of shooting, all you have to do is divide the number of shots made by the number of shots of that type attempted and multiply the result by 100. Field goal percentages are usually listed first, followed by free throw percentage and then 3-point shooting percentage. These numbers are often given as decimals, such as .482. To convert the decimal to a percentage, just move the decimal point two places to the right. In this case, the .482 is 48.2%.

The box score for the Boston-New York matchup shows only 3-point shooting, so we'll figure out a percentage for that. In that game, Boston made 3 out of 4 3-point shots. Dividing 3 by 4 and multiplying by 100, we find that the Celtics made 75% of their 3-point shots. The Knicks, however, made only 2 out of 11 attempts, for a percentage of .182, or 18.2%.

After the 3-point stats, the names of players who attempted at least one 3-point shot are listed in parentheses, along with how many shots they actually made. In the game against Boston, for example, we see that 5 New York players attempted 3-point shots but only 2, Ewing and Starks, were successful.

The next information in this area of the long form concerns **team rebounds.** A team rebound is given to a team when a ball that was shot at the basket bounces off the rim or backboard and goes out of bounds before it can be grabbed by a player on either team. The team that did not touch the ball last before it went out of bounds is then given possession of the ball and is credited with a team rebound. New York had 14 team rebounds, Boston had 9.

After team rebounds come **blocked shots.** A blocked

shot (also called a block, rejection, or stuff) is awarded to a player who deflects a shot at the basket with his hand or arm without the ball going in, without a foul being called on the blocking player, and without the referee calling a **goaltending** violation. Goaltending violations are usually called on a player for swatting a ball away while it is on its way down toward the basket or for touching a ball while it is on the rim and knocking it out. Blocks are presented in the box score just like 3-pointers. After the team total, all the players who blocked at least one shot are listed. Looking at the long form, we see that the Knicks had 5 blocked shots, 3 by Ewing and one each by Mason and Anthony. Boston had 7, with one shot blocked by Fox, and Gamble, Parish, and Lewis each blocking two shots.

Turnovers and **steals** finish up this section of the long form, and these are listed in the same way as blocked shots. A turnover occurs when a player loses the ball for his team by throwing the ball out of bounds, throwing the ball to a player on the other team, or losing control of the ball while dribbling, or because of a violation. Steals are given to players who catch passes that were intended for an opposing player or who take the ball away from an opposing player while he is dribbling.

Next there may be listings for **technical fouls**—which are given for very illegal actions like punching another player, swearing, or yelling at a referee—and **flagrant fouls,** which are given when players engage in play that is rougher than necessary. In both cases, the player or team guilty of technical or flagrant fouls is listed, along with the quarter in which the foul occurred and the time that had elapsed in that period when the call was made.

To finish out the long form, scores are listed by quarter. This means that you will see five numbers for each team (in a standard game). The first number indicates how many points the team scored in the first quarter of the game; the second number, how many were scored in the second quarter; and so on for the third and fourth quarters. The last number is the total number of points the team scored during the game. In the game against Boston, New York scored 22 points in the first quarter, 23 in the second, 20 in the third, and 24 in the fourth, for a total of 89 points.

Finally, the attendance figure (A), the time the game took to play (T), and the names of the three game referees are at the very bottom of the long form. There were 14,890 people at the New York-Boston game, which lasted 2 hours and 6 minutes. The three referees were Ed T. Rush, Jim Kinsey, and Greg Willard.

INDIVIDUAL PLAYER STATISTICS

Statistics for individual basketball players on both college and professional teams are the same stats that appear in basketball box scores, totaled and averaged throughout the season. For example, to get a player's average number of assists per game, add the number of assists a player has during the season and divide it by the number of games he has played in.

Basketball players are ranked according to all sorts of statistical averages: Points, rebounds, steals, blocks, and assists are a few of them. Percentages are also important. People want to know how well players shoot the ball, and they want to know how well they do it from a variety of places on the court. To find a percentage, you just have to divide the total shots completed by the number attempted and multiply by 100. For example, to find a player's field goal percentage, you divide the total number of field goals he made during the season by the number he attempted and multiply the result by 100.

Height is another very important factor in basketball. Height is one way that coaches determine what position a player should cover. In general, taller players should play the forward and center positions on a team, while shorter players are expected to be good at the two guard positions. Over the years, taller players have tended to perform better in rebounding and shot blocking, while shorter players usually do better in assists and steals. The NBA's tallest player, Manute Bol, stands nearly 7' 7" tall. The shortest player in the league is Tyrone "Mugsy" Bogues, who stands about 5' 3". Not surprisingly, Bol is almost always among the leaders in blocked shots per game, averaging 3.0 per game in 1991. Bogues, a guard for the Charlotte Hornets, passes and steals very well. He averaged 8.3 assists and 1.7 steals per game in 1991.

Sometimes, though, players we wouldn't expect to do well in certain categories because of their size do quite well anyway. For example, Charles Barkley of Philadelphia might not seem like the best rebounder in the world, since he is only 6' 5". Yet in 1987 Barkley led the NBA in rebounding, with 14.6 per game. Wilt Chamberlain, who stands 7' 1", was one of the most ferocious rebounders and scorers in the history of basketball, holding the NBA record for the most points in a single game: 100. But Chamberlain also once led the league in assists, with 8.6 per game in 1968.

Now you've seen how two of the most popular sports in the world determine their statistics. But get ready: You're about to explore the world of football statistics.

That's where things get interesting.

3.   FOOTBALL

*F*ootball coaches, announcers, reporters, and fans have a lot of numbers to collect and compare if they want to keep up with the sport. To make matters even more complicated, with one exception, each type of player on the field has his own set of statistics. Receivers have different stats from running backs, and quarterbacks have stats all their own. Only offensive linemen don't have statistics, and that's only because they rarely touch the ball during a game!

FOOTBALL STANDINGS

Like baseball and basketball, football teams are divided into two conferences, the American Football Conference (AFC) and the National Football Conference (NFC). Each conference is subdivided into divisions, which are used to help simplify the complicated football playoff system, which could use a book of its own. Each conference has an Eastern, Central, and Western division, and, as in other sports, teams that come from cities in the East are in the Eastern Division, teams from the West make up the Western Division, and teams from the central states form the Central Division. There are a few exceptions to this rule: The Atlanta Falcons are in the NFC Western Division, for example, because there are more teams from eastern cities than from western cities.

Overall football standings are somewhat different from those we looked at for baseball and basketball. Because football games can end in ties, there will be a column for these, in addition to wins and losses. There are also two columns labeled **PF** and **PA.** These stand for **points for** and **points against.** These numbers tell us the number of points a team has scored during the season and the number of points a team has allowed opposing teams to score during the season.

Look at the sample standings chart below. As you can

NFL

AMERICAN CONFERENCE

East

	W	L	T	Pct.	PF	PA
Buffalo	9	1	0	.900	301	211
Jets	6	5	0	.545	231	206
Miami	5	5	0	.500	180	207
New England	3	8	0	.273	156	223
Indianapolis	1	10	0	.091	106	261

Central

	W	L	T	Pct.	PF	PA
Houston	9	2	0	.818	298	168
Cleveland	4	7	0	.364	211	232
Pittsburgh	4	7	0	.364	216	259
Cincinnati	1	10	0	.091	170	312

West

	W	L	T	Pct.	PF	PA
Denver	8	3	0	.727	216	179
Kansas City	7	4	0	.636	227	160
LA Raiders	7	4	0	.636	203	192
Seattle	5	6	0	.455	199	173
San Diego	3	8	0	.273	195	242

NATIONAL CONFERENCE

East

	W	L	T	Pct.	PF	PA
x-Washington	11	0	0	1.000	361	139
Philadelphia	6	5	0	.545	182	163
Dallas	6	5	0	.545	219	225
Giants	6	5	0	.545	181	183
Phoenix	4	8	0	.333	146	239

Central

	W	L	T	Pct.	PF	PA
Chicago	9	2	0	.818	212	172
Detroit	7	4	0	.636	217	224
Minnesota	6	6	0	.500	234	207
Green Bay	2	9	0	.182	171	213
Tampa Bay	2	9	0	.182	130	255

West

	W	L	T	Pct.	PF	PA
New Orleans	9	2	0	.818	229	124
Atlanta	6	5	0	.545	219	229
San Francisco	5	6	0	.455	218	155
LA Rams	3	8	0	.273	181	256

see, there are listings for both the AFC and the NFC. Within these listings, the teams are arranged according to division. In the American Conference's Central Division, the Houston Oilers hold the top spot. Looking at their stats, we see that, at this point in the season, they have won 9 games and lost 2. None of their games have ended in ties. This record gives Houston a winning percentage of .818. Again, the higher a team's winning percentage, the better they are performing. The Washington Redskins of the National Conference's Eastern Division have a winning percentage of 1.0, the best in either conference and the best percentage a team can have. This means that they have won every game they played.

Looking at the PF and PA column, we can see how many points Houston has scored and given up during the season so far. In 11 games, the Oilers managed to score 298 points, while allowing opposing teams to score only 168. Points for and points against have no bearing on a team's winning percentage, but they may be used to compare teams with similar winning percentages. For example, the Houston Oilers, Chicago Bears, and New Orleans Saints each have a winning percentage of .818: Each has won 9 and lost 2 games. But over those 11 games, the Oilers earned 298 points, compared to 212 for the Bears and 229 for the Saints.

BOX SCORES

In a typical box score for a football game, the first two lines indicate the teams that played the game, the score by quarters, and the final score, just as you would find in a basketball or baseball box score. The visiting team is on the top line, the home team on the bottom. The box score on page 52 contains information about a game between the Chicago Bears and the Indianapolis Colts.

Because the Bears are listed on top, we know that they

BEARS 31, COLTS 17

Chicago	7 3 14 7—31	
Indianapolis	7 3 0 7—17	

First Quarter
Ind—Hester 4 pass from George (Biasucci kick), 6:59.
Chi—Harbaugh 6 run (Butler kick), 12:34
Second Quarter
Chi—FG Butler 21, 13:06.
Ind—FG Biasucci 56, 14:57.
Third Quarter
Chi—Muster 13 pass from Harbaugh (Butler kick), 8:26.
Chi—Morgan 84 pass from Harbaugh (Butler kick), 11:22.
Fourth Quarter
Ind—Brooks 9 pass from George (Biasucci kick), :07.
Chi—Muster 9 run (Butler kick), 13:04.
A—60,519

	Chi	Ind
First downs	27	14
Rushes-yards	32-175	19-111
Passing	273	140
Return Yards	39	15
Comp-Att-Int	18-32-1	16-33-0
Sacked-Yards Lost	3-14	5-36
Punts	3-42	7-45
Fumbles-Lost	1-1	0-0
Penalties-Yards	5-42	6-65
Time of Possession	36:31	23:29

INDIVIDUAL STATISTICS
RUSHING—Chicago, Muster 15-101, Green 9-53, Bailey 6-14, Harbaugh 2-7. Indianapolis, Clark 11-67, Manoa 6-26, George 2-18.
PASSING—Chicago, Harbaugh 18-32-1-287. Indianapolis, George 16-33-0-176.
RECEIVING—Chicago, Muster 6-44, Davis 3-50, Thornton 2-47, Gentry 2-25, Waddle 2-21, Morgan 1-84, Jennings 1-12, Green 1-4. Indianapolis, Brooks 7-106, Hester 4-32, Clark 3-11, Martin 1-25, Verdin 1-2.
MISSED FIELD GOALS—None.

were the visiting team and that the game was played in Indianapolis. The numbers to the right of the team names indicate the score by quarters for the game. In this game, both teams scored 7 points in the first quarter and 3 points in the second quarter, which means that they were tied at halftime. In the third quarter, Chicago scored 14 points, while Indianapolis scored none. Finally, both teams scored 7 points in the fourth and final quarter of the game.

After the basic score by quarter there is a detailed scoring summary that tells how each team scored its points in each quarter. The team name comes first, followed by the names of players who scored points, the distance in yards that the play covered, what the play was, and how many minutes into the quarter the score occurred.

In the first quarter of the Chicago-Indianapolis game, we can see that Hester of Indianapolis scored first on a 4-yard pass from George. This gave the Colts 6 points. They added another when Biasucci made the **extra point.** In professional football, when a team makes a touchdown it is allowed to try for an extra point. This is sometimes called a point after touchdown, or PAT. This means that the ball is placed on the 2-yard line and the team that scored the touchdown gets a chance to kick the ball through the goalposts into the endzone, which results in an additional point.

In college football, a successful kick is also worth one point. But in a college game, the team has the option of running or passing the ball into the end zone. If successful, the team is awarded 2 points. This is called a **2-point conversion.** In both pro or college football, if a 2-yard play doesn't work, no points are given.

In the second quarter of the Bears-Colts game, both teams scored 3 points. Because the score is under 6 points, we know that neither team scored a touchdown. This means that they must have scored **field goals.** A field goal is when a player kicks the football between the goalposts. A team usually tries for a field goal when it is the fourth down and the team doesn't think it can advance the ball far enough to get another set of downs or when time in a quarter is running out and they are too far away from the end zone to be likely to make a touchdown. Like touchdowns, stats for field goals show who kicked the field goal, how many yards he kicked it, and at what point in the period the field goal occurred. Butler of Chicago made the first field goal of the second quarter, kicking the ball 21 yards. Biasucci of Indianapolis kicked the second field goal almost 15 minutes into the quarter. He kicked the ball 56 yards.

After all four quarters are listed, you will see a figure for attendance at the game. There were 60,519 fans at the game between the Bears and the Colts.

TEAM STATISTICS

After the scoring summary, several team statistics are presented. They are all labeled and put into columns by team. The visiting team is shown on the left, the home team on the right.

First downs: the number of times the team gained a new set of downs. In football a team gets four chances, or plays, to move the football ten yards toward its opponent's end zone. When the team first takes possession of the ball, or successfully achieves a first down, it has four plays to advance the ball ten yards from its original position. From play to play, you will hear announcers say a down number and a number of yards, such as 2nd and 7. This means that the team is on its second play and needs seven more yards to get another first down and four more plays. If a team fails to gain ten yards on the four plays, the ball is turned over to the other team.

Rushes-yards: the number of running plays a team attempted and the total yardage those plays gained.

Passing yards: the number of yards a team gained through passing plays.

Return yards: the yardage gained by punt, kickoff, and interception returns.

Comp-Att-Int refers to two things. Comp-Att is the number of passing plays completed compared to the number attempted. The third number listed here, Int, represents the number of **interceptions** the team threw. An interception occurs when a defensive player catches a pass intended for an offensive player.

Sacked-yards lost: the number of times a team allowed its quarterback to be tackled behind the yard line from which the play started, followed by the yardage lost by those sacks.

Punts: the number of punts in the game and the average distance of each.

Fumbles-lost: the number of times a team fumbled, or dropped, the ball and the other team recovered it.

Penalties-yards: the number of penalties committed by the team and the total yardage lost as a result.

Finally, **time of possession** is the total time that the team held the ball during the game.

INDIVIDUAL PLAYER STATISTICS

The final section, **individual statistics,** is concerned with four things: what the action during the game was, which player performed it, how many times he did it, and what he accomplished.

The first type of action listed is **rushing.** This stat tells us who gained yards for a team on running plays. A running play is any time a player carries a ball down the field and advances his team. The rushing statistic will list the player's name, followed by how many times he carried the ball for his team and how far he got with it. In the box score for the Chicago-Indianapolis game, Muster of Chicago is the first player listed in the section on rushing.

He carried the ball 15 times during the game and ran for a total of 101 yards.

If you add up all of the rushing stats for a team, the total number should equal the rushes-yards stat that we saw earlier in the box score. For example, Clark, Manoa, and George of the Colts carried the ball 19 times (11 + 6 + 2) for a total of 111 yards (67 + 26 + 18). If we look under the **rushes-yards** column for Indianapolis, we see 19-111.

The second section in the individual stats is **passing.** Passing stats are concerned with one player on a team: the quarterback. The quarterback is probably the most important player on a football team. Coaches, reporters, and fans have to keep track of a huge amount of quarterback statistics. In the passing section, you will see the names of the quarterbacks who played in the game, followed by 4 numbers. These numbers represent the number of completed passes a quarterback made, the number of passes attempted, the number of interceptions thrown, and the total yardage gained through a quarterback's passing.

Look at the passing stats for the showdown between the Bears and the Colts. Chicago's quarterback, Harbaugh, has the numbers 18-32-1-287 after his name. This means that he threw 18 passes that were completed out of a total of 32 attempts. One of his passes was intercepted by an Indianapolis player. He gave up one interception. The 18 completed passes that Harbaugh threw allowed the Bears to advance 287 yards.

The final section found in the individual statistics is **receiving.** The stats in this section are arranged just like the ones in the rushing section. A player's name is listed, followed by the number of times the player caught a thrown ball and how much yardage he picked up. For example, Muster of Chicago caught 6 passes for a total of 44 yards.

COMPUTING STATISTICS FROM BOX SCORE INFORMATION

There are some stats used to compare football players that won't be found in a box score but that can easily be computed using the information from the box score. Once you know how to do this, it is easy to make up stats to compare your favorite players and teams.

STATISTICS FOR QUARTERBACKS

By using the basic numbers given in a box score for how a quarterback performed during a game, we can come up with many different stats that show how well a player performed. One such stat is the **completion percentage.** This is simply the number of completed passes a quarterback has, divided by the number of passes he attempts. For example, to find the completion percentage for Harbaugh of the Bears, we would simply divide his completed passes (18) by his attempted passes (32) and multiply by 100. This gives him a completion percentage of 56.25 for the game against the Colts. If we know a quarterback's totals for a season, we can figure out a completion percentage for a season and even his entire career.

Another important quarterback stat you can figure out using the basic box score information is **average gain per pass attempt.** This stat has a long name, but it really is very simple. What it tells us is the average yardage each of the quarterback's throws allows his team to advance. For example, George of the Colts threw for 176 yards in 33 attempts. Dividing the yards (176) by the attempts (33), we find he gained an average of 5.3 yards per attempt.

Touchdown percentage is similar to completion percentage. It measures what percentage of a quarterback's throws result in touchdowns. This stat is computed by dividing the number of pass attempts into the number of passes that result in touchdowns. To find out how many of a quarterback's passes result in touchdowns, you have to refer to the scoring summary in the first section of the box score. If a score is followed by the words "pass from George," for example, we know that the touchdown was a result of a pass thrown by George. Looking at the scoring summary for the Bears–Colts game, we see that George threw two touchdown passes in his 33 attempts, so his touchdown percentage would be .06, or 6%.

Coaches want quarterbacks who don't throw interceptions, so naturally they have developed a stat that shows how often a quarterback's throws are intercepted. It is called **interception percentage,** and it is computed exactly like touchdown percentage: by dividing the number of interceptions by the number of pass attempts. Harbaugh of the Bears had one interception in 32 attempts, so his interception percentage would be 3%.

Besides passing skills, quarterbacks are sometimes compared using skills such as the ability to run for yards. But to thoroughly compare different quarterbacks, a statistic called the **quarterback rating** was developed by two mathematicians at the Massachusetts Institute of Technology. Exactly how and why the formula works is far too complicated to explain, but using the formula is very easy. Quarterback rating is used for both college and professional players, but it is most often used for professionals, so we will look only at the pro version.

First, take the quarterback completion percentage we learned about earlier and subtract 30 from it. Then divide that number by 20. We will call this number A. Now take the quarterback's average gain per pass attempt stat, subtract 3 from it, and divide the result by 4. This is number B. To find C, take the touchdown percentage and divide it by 5. Finally, subtract the quarterback's interception percentage from 9.5 and divide the result by 4 to get number D. Add A, B, C, and D together, divide the total by 6, and multiply that result by 100. The number you get will be the quarterback rating for the player you are looking at.

Let's figure the quarterback rating for Harbaugh, the quarterback for the Bears in the game we have been examining in this chapter. We already figured out Harbaugh's completion percentage, which was 56.25. Subtract 30 from this and we get 26.25. Dividing 26.25 by 20, we find that number A is 1.3.

Number B is based on average gain, so we must compute Harbaugh's average gain percentage from box score information. He threw 32 passes for a total of 287 yards, so by dividing 287 by 32, we get an average gain per pass attempt of 8.96, or 9. To get B, we subtract 3 from 9 (6) and divide by 4, for a total of 1.5.

Getting number C is a little trickier. Look back at the scoring summary by quarter. In the third quarter, we see that Muster scored 2 touchdowns on passes from Harbaugh. That means that 2 of Harbaugh's 32 passes resulted in touchdowns. Using the formula for computing touchdown percentage, we get Harbaugh's percentage of 6.25 (2 divided by 32 multiplied by 100). To get number C, we divide 6.25 by 5, getting 1.25.

Harbaugh's interception percentage is needed for number D. We already computed that earlier, so we know it is 3. Subtracting that from 9.5, we get 6.5. Dividing 6.5 by 4, we get a result of 1.6.

Now that we have all of our base numbers, we can get down to figuring out Harbaugh's quarterback rating. We add A (1.3), B (1.5), C (1.25), and D (1.6), for a total of 5.65. Dividing this by 6 and multiplying by 100, we get Harbaugh's quarterback rating of 94.2. Finding a quarterback rating is a lot of work, but it is a useful number to know, and it also shows how you can use the basic information found in a box score to learn more about the players.

INDIVIDUAL STATISTICS FOR OTHER PLAYERS

Quarterbacks aren't the only players on a football team that have stats. You can easily compute stats for any player on a team by using the formulas we have already learned. For example, if you want to find a player's rushing average, you now know that all you have to do is divide the total number of yards he gained by the total number of rushes he attempted.

And let's not forget defensive players' statistics. Defensive players (players who are on the field while the other team has the ball) can have **tackles, assists, tackles for a loss, sacks, interceptions, interception return yardage, fumble recoveries,** and **fumble return yardage.**

A player is credited with a tackle when he knocks an opposing player carrying the football to the ground or out of bounds. He gets an assist if he helps tackle the player but is not the only player involved in the tackle. A tackle for a loss is when a defensive player stops a ball carrier other than the quarterback behind the **line of scrimmage.** This is the yardline on which the play started. If the player he stops is the quarterback, this is called a sack.

Interceptions, as we discussed earlier, are when a player catches a ball that was meant for a player on the other team. Interception return yardage is the yardage the defensive player who caught the interception runs with the ball after catching it.

A fumble recovery is when a player picks up or falls on a ball that is dropped by a player on the opposing team. Fumble return yardage is the yardage he gains after picking up the fumbled ball.

USING FOOTBALL STATISTICS

In the introduction, we learned how statistics are used to help us keep track of the best and worst performances of all time. We can do the same thing in football.

As in all other sports, football fans are mainly concerned with a team's won-loss record. Looking at a team's won-loss record over a season or over several seasons can tell us a lot about the team. In college football, the Columbia University Lions hold an interesting place in the won-loss category. Playing 10 games a season, the Columbia Lions didn't win a single game in over 4 years! Finally, on October 8, 1988, the Lions ended their record 44-game losing streak by defeating the Princeton Tigers 16-13.

While winning streaks are fairly common in college ball, they are very unusual in professional football. Only one team in NFL history, the 1972 Miami Dolphins, have had an undefeated record, 14-0-0. In 1978 the NFL switched to a 16-game schedule, and no teams have gone undefeated since then.

Individual players also hold interesting records. Tom Dempsey, a former kicker with the New Orleans Saints, holds the record for the longest field goal ever kicked by a professional player. Playing against the Detroit Lions in 1970, Dempsey kicked a 63-yard field goal. What makes his feat even more special is that Dempsey was born without his right hand and with several toes missing from his kicking foot.

This brings up another area of football that has several stats: kicking. When punters and kickers kick the ball, we measure how far they kick it. But this distance can sometimes be confusing. Field goals are measured from the spot that they are kicked from. But because all goalposts are 10 yards behind the goalline in the end zone, we add 10 yards to the distance of any field goal kicked. Suppose, for example, a team attempts a field goal from the 29-yard line. The kicker actually kicks the ball from the 36-yard line, since kickers tend to place the ball 7 yards behind the line of scrimmage to prevent a block by the defense. Since the goalposts are 10 yards behind the goalline, the actual distance is 46 yards.

Punts are much simpler. Even though most punters kick the ball from 10 to 15 yards behind the line of scrimmage, the distance of a punt is measured from the line of scrimmage.

Punters have other stats that you might find in a newspaper or see on a television broadcast. **Average distance** is simply how far a punter punts the ball, on average. To find this stat, you just divide the total yards punted by the number of punts attempted.

Average hang time is a measure of how long a kicker's punt stays, or hangs, in the air. The longer a ball is in the air, the more time defensive players have to run down the field and get an opportunity to tackle the player who is catching the punt. There is also a punt stat called **net yardage.** This is the yards a kicker punts, minus the yards that the opposing team runs once they catch the punt. For example, if a punter kicks the ball 60 yards, but the other team catches the ball and runs it back for 35 yards, the net yardage for the punt is only 25 yards.

A football box score looks deceptively simple at first, but now you know how many different stats can be computed from the information given in that small amount of space. If you can figure out quarterback ratings, rushing averages, and net yardage, give yourself a pat on the back. It's not easy stuff.

4. HOCKEY
AND TENNIS

*W*hile baseball, basketball, and football are three main sports written about in newspapers, it wouldn't be fair to other popular sports that are played around the world if we didn't mention their statistics. So let's take a look at two other popular sports you might see listed on a sports page: hockey and tennis.

HOCKEY STANDINGS

The National Hockey League (NHL) was created in 1917. Games are played in many cities in North America, and, of course, statistics are kept. The standings for hockey are a little different than those for other sports. Wins and losses are still recorded, but since hockey games can end in ties, these are also given. Rather than base the standings for hockey on wins and losses, we rank the teams according to a system of **points.** Teams are given 2 points for every win that they get, one point for every tie, and none for a loss.

Look at the example of hockey standings given on page 64. As in other sports, you will see that hockey teams are divided up into two conferences, the Wales Conference and the Campbell Conference, and four divisions, the Patrick, Adams, Norris, and Smythe divisions. In the Patrick Division, the Washington Capitals are in first

NHL

WALES CONFERENCE
Patrick Division

	W	L	T	Pts	GF	GA
Washington	15	4	0	30	96	57
Rangers	12	8	1	25	70	65
Devils	11	9	0	22	73	56
Pittsburgh	8	8	3	19	72	77
Philadelphia	8	9	1	17	53	52
Islanders	6	10	2	14	64	76

Adams Division

	W	L	T	Pts	GF	GA
Montreal	14	6	2	30	73	38
Hartford	9	7	3	21	61	61
Boston	7	7	4	18	64	62
Buffalo	7	9	2	16	50	59
Quebec	3	14	1	7	55	81

CAMPBELL CONFERENCE
Norris Division

	W	L	T	Pts	GF	GA
Chicago	10	7	5	25	80	69
Detroit	11	8	2	24	84	70
St. Louis	8	8	5	21	65	75
Minnesota	8	9	1	17	60	60
Toronto	5	14	3	13	51	78

Smythe Division

	W	L	T	Pts	GF	GA
Vancouver	14	4	3	31	81	51
Winnipeg	9	8	4	22	61	65
Calgary	9	8	3	21	80	67
Los Angeles	8	7	5	21	72	79
Edmonton	7	11	3	17	66	81
San Jose	3	17	1	7	52	104

place. They have 15 wins, 4 losses, and no ties, for a total of 30 points.

Next to the column for total points, you will find columns labeled GF and GA. The numbers listed here represent the total number of goals a team has scored during the season (**goals for**) and the total number of goals the team has allowed other teams to score (**goals against**). This stat is similar to the points for and points against stat in football. The Washington Capitals have scored a total of 96 goals during the season and allowed other teams to score 57 goals.

BOX SCORES

Hockey box scores are a little different, too. A hockey game is usually divided into 3 20-minute periods. If the score is tied after the first 3 periods then a fourth, or overtime, period is played. This overtime period lasts 5 minutes. If neither team scores during this period, the game ends in a tie, unless the game is a playoff game, in which case more overtimes are played.

The box score on page 66 is for a game between the Vancouver Canucks and the Winnipeg Jets. As in football, the visiting team is listed first. Then there is a scoring summary by period. In this game, the Jets scored only 2 goals during the game, both of them in the second period. The Canucks scored 8 goals, 2 in the first period, 4 in the second, and 2 in the third.

Following the scoring summary is a breakdown of the action in each period. As in a football summary, the goals are listed in the order in which they occurred. The player scoring the goal is shown, along with a number indicating his total goals for the season. Next to that number will be parentheses with the names of up to 2 other players. These players are credited with assists on the goal. In hockey, as in other sports, an assist is given when a player makes a pass that helps beat the defense and allows another player to score a goal. In this case, a player passes the hockey puck to another player, allowing him to get it into the net. Since not all goals are made on assists, you will not always find names in parentheses. The final number listed is the amount of time in the period that had elapsed when the goal was made.

For example, the first goal scored in the Canucks-Jets matchup was made by Vancouver. Bure made the goal, bringing his season total to 2. Larionov and Momesso assisted Bure in making the goal, and it occurred 17 minutes and 30 seconds into the game.

Canucks 8, Jets 2

Winnipeg	0	2	0—2
Vancouver	2	4	2—8

First Period—1, Vancouver, Bure 2 (Larionov, Momesso), 17:30. 2, Vancouver, Sandlak 2 (Bure, Adams), 19:56 (pp). Penalties—Shannon, Win (tripping), :33; Gregg, Van (crosschecking), :33; Tkachuk, Win (interference), 2:28; Dirk, Van (hooking), 9:54; Steen, Win (hooking), 13:15; Momesso, Van, misconduct, 17:30; Ulanov, Win (holding), 19:22.

Second Period—3, Vancouver, Babych 1 (Larionov, McLean), :35. 4, Vancouver, Lumme 2 (Linden, Bure), 2:28 (pp). 5, Vancouver, Nedved 1 (Babych), 7:20. 6, Vancouver, Lidster 1 (Larionov, Bure), 8:59. 7, Winnipeg, Olczyk 2 (Davydov), 16:24. 8, Winnipeg, Broten 2 (Shannon, Elynuik), 17:21. Penalties—Lalor, Win (cross-checking), :55; Carlyle, Win (elbowing), 2:10; Sandlak, Van (hooking), 4:55; Cronin, Win (high-sticking), 10:14; Nedved, Van, misconduct, 10:14; Bure, Van (charging), 12:42; Tkachuk, Win, minor-misconduct (high-sticking), 14:07; Dirk, Van (roughing), 14:07.

Third Period—9, Vancouver, Sandlak 3 (Nedved, Fergus), 1:49. 10, Vancouver, Courtnall 1 (Walter, Gregg), 10:22. Penalties—Shannon, Win (tripping), 2:52; Momesso, Van (high-sticking), 5:13; Tkachuk, Win (roughing), 17:32; Dirk, Van (roughing), 17:32; Linden, Van (charging), 17:32.

Shots on goal—Winnipeg 7-8-11—26. Vancouver 19-11-13—43. Power-play Opportunities—Winnipeg 0 of 5; Vancouver 2 of 7. Goalies—Winnipeg, Tabaracci, 3-2 (26 shots-21 saves), Essensa, (7:20 second, 17-14). Vancouver, McLean, 2-3 (26-24). A—16,123. Referee—Andy vanHellemond. Linesmen—Jerry Pateman, Gerard Gauthier.

If a goal was scored on a **power play, shorthanded situation,** or against an **empty net,** there will be an additional set of parentheses with an abbreviation for one of these situations in it. Power plays, labeled **PP,** occur when the defensive team has fewer players than the goal-scoring team because one or more of their players is off the ice because of committing **penalties.** Empty net goals (**EN**) happen when the team that gave up the goal removed their goaltender from play and replaced him with an additional player in an attempt to create a more powerful offensive team. Shorthanded goals (**SH**) occur when a team is able to score a goal despite having fewer players than the team it scored against. Looking at the Vancouver-Winnipeg box score, we see that 2 of the 10 goals of the game were scored on power plays, one in the first period and one in the second.

The penalties that occurred in each period are listed after goals scored. The name of the player who committed the penalty is given, along with the type of penalty in parentheses and the time into the period when the penalty was called. Penalties normally last for 2 to 5 minutes, although some really violent play can force a player out of a game or suspend him for several games. There are many different types of penalties that can be called. The most common ones are listed below.

Hooking: when a player trips another player on purpose.

Cross-checking: lifting the stick off the ice and using it to block an opposing player.

High sticking: when a player holds his stick over his shoulder.

Slashing: hitting an opposing player with a stick.

Other common penalties, easily explained by their names, are **elbowing, roughing, fighting,** and **interference.**

In the game that we have been studying, there were quite a few penalties called. In the first period, 7 players were given penalties, including Tkachuk of Winnipeg for interference and Momesso of Vancouver for misconduct.

After the information about scoring and penalties, there is a section devoted to stats for the entire game. The first stat given is for **shots on goal.** This stat simply tells you how many times a team tried to score during a game. Shots on goal is divided into periods, with a total given at the end. The shots on goal line for the game between the Canucks and the Jets reads "Winnipeg 7-8-11—26." This tells us that the Jets made 7 shots at the goal in the first period, 8 in the second, and 11 in the final period, for a total of 26 attempted goals.

After shots by goal, any penalty shots taken by the teams are listed, along with the names of the players attempting them, the time they were attempted, and whether or not they were successful. There may also be a listing for power play opportunities for both teams. This stat shows how many times a team was in a power play situation, which we discussed earlier, and whether or not they were able to score during the play. In our sample game, the Jets had 5 opportunities to score on power plays but were not successful on any of them. In contrast, the Canucks had 7 opportunities and scored twice.

The next set of stats belongs to the goalies for each team. Each goaltender who played in the game will be listed. His name will be followed by his won-loss record for the season. Then in parentheses, there will be a set of numbers showing how many shots were attempted against him and how many he stopped.

Look at the goaltender stats for the Canuck-Jets game. The first goalie listed, Tabaracci of Winnipeg, has a 3–2 won-loss record for the current hockey season. There were 26 goals attempted against him, and he saved 21 of them. This means that he allowed 5 goals while he was in the game. Winnipeg also had a second goaltender, Essensa. By looking at the information in parentheses after Essensa's name, we see that he entered the game 7 minutes and 20 seconds into the second period. During the rest of the game, 17 shots were made against him, 14 of which he blocked. This means he allowed 3 shots to get into the net. If you add this to the 5 goals that Tabaracci gave up, you get a total of 8, the final score for the Canucks. McLean of Vancouver played the entire game. The Canucks' win gave him a new won-loss record of 2 wins and 3 losses. There were 26 goals attempted against McLean, 24 of which he prevented.

After all the goalie stats, attendance for the game is listed, along with the names of the referee and the **linesmen** who officiated at the matchup.

INDIVIDUAL PLAYER STATISTICS

While you won't usually find individual player stats on a sports page, you might hear them given during games or see them flashed on television, so it's a good idea to be familiar with them.

Players other than goalies usually have 6 statistics that people keep track of: **goals, assists, points, +/- rating, PIM,** and **PP.**

Goals are simply the number of goals that a player has scored during the season. Similarly, assists are the number of times a player has helped another teammate score a goal. Scoring ability is measured by points. This stat is the sum total of goals and assists.

The next stat, +/-, is more complicated. As its name indicates, this number can be either positive or negative. It measures the number of goals scored by the player's team while he is on the ice, minus the number of goals given up by his team while he is on the ice. However, goals scored by the player's team during a power play or goals allowed by the player's team when it is shorthanded do not count in the +/- stat. Goals scored by the team when it is shorthanded or against the team while the team is on a power play do count, but goals scored while a player is off the ice do not.

Let's say that Mark Messier of the New York Rangers has been on the ice while his team has scored 30 goals, 5 of which were scored on power plays. During this time, the Rangers allowed other teams to score 29 goals, 10 of which came while the Rangers were shorthanded. To find Messier's +/- rating, we first find the total number of goals scored by the Rangers while he was on the ice. This would be 30 minus the 5 power play goals, or 25. Then we find the total number of goals scored against the Rangers. This would be 29 minus the 10 scored while the Rangers were shorthanded, or 19. Finally, we subtract the goals scored against (19) from the goals scored (25) to get Messier's +/- rating of 6. The higher a +/- rating is on the positive side, the better it is.

PIM, or penalties in minutes, is the total number of penalty minutes that a player has gotten during the season. Depending on the type of penalty they commit, players spend various amounts of time in the penalty box. But sometimes a player will not spend the full amount of time in the penalty box. If a goal is scored, or if the time remaining in the game is less than the length of his penalty, a player may get out of the penalty box early. In PIM, however, the length of time a penalty is actually worth is counted, regardless of whether or not the player actually sat in the penalty box for that length of time.

PP, or power play goals, is the number of power play goals a player has scored during a season.

Sometimes you may hear an announcer use the term **hat trick.** A hat trick occurs when a player scores 3 or more goals in a game. On the third goal, the player is said to have scored a hat trick. If he scores three goals in a row, he has scored a **natural hat trick.** Why are they called hat tricks? Fans sometimes toss their hats out onto the ice whenever a player scores three goals in a game.

GOALTENDING STATISTICS

For goalies, hockey fans keep track of the usual won-loss record and saves. Fans also keep track of **shutouts.** A shutout occurs whenever a goalie plays an entire game and does not allow any goals to be scored against him.

Goalies also have statistics for **save percentage** and **goals against average.** To find save percentage, all you have to do is divide a goalie's total number of saves by the sum of his saves plus goals allowed. For example, let's find the save percentage for McLean, the goalie for the Canucks in the game against the Jets. McLean had 24 saves during the game out of 26 attempted shots, letting 2 goals score. To find his save percentage, we divide the number of saves (24) by the sum of saves plus goals made (24 + 2 = 26), for a save percentage of 92.3 for the game.

For goals against average, we measure the number of goals allowed by the goalie per minute he spent on the ice. This is a little bit like earned run average in baseball. To find goals against average, multiply the number of goals the goalie allowed by 60 (the total number of minutes in a standard hockey game) and divide it by the number of minutes the goalie played in the game. To find the goals against average for McLean, we multiply the number of goals he allowed the Jets to make (2) by 60, for 120. We then divide that by 60, since McLean played the entire game and there was no overtime. This gives McLean a goals against average of 2, which is very good.

Now let's find the goals against average for Tabaracci of Winnipeg. This is a little trickier, because we know he didn't play the entire game against Vancouver. We already know that Tabaracci allowed 5 goals. Multiply that by 60, to get 300. Now we have to find the total number of minutes that Tabaracci played. We see that he was replaced by Essensa 7 minutes and 20 seconds into the second period. This means that he played one full period of 20 minutes, plus the 7 minutes and 20 seconds of the second period, for a total of 27 minutes and 20 seconds. Because 20 seconds is exactly one-third of a minute, we can say that Tabaracci played for 27.33 minutes. Now we can divide 300 by 27.33, for a goals against average of 10.9.

Excellent goalies will have a high save percentage and low goals against average.

TENNIS

Tennis is a popular game all over the world. While its statistics are completely different from those found in any other sport, they are not difficult to understand with a little bit of explanation.

BOX SCORES

When results of a tennis match are listed in the newspaper, they are presented in the manner shown below.

ATP Championships

YESTERDAY'S RESULTS
At Frankfurt, Germany
Championship
Pete Sampras (6), Bradenton, Fla., def. Jim Courier (1), Dade City, Fla., 3-6, 7-6 (7-5), 6-3, 6-4

The winner's name is listed first, with her or his overall ranking in the tennis tournament, called her or his **seeding,** in parentheses. You will then see the name of the player's hometown, or country if she or he is not from the United States. This information will be followed by the abbreviation **def.** for "defeated." Then the information about the player who lost the match will be given.

The game shown in the diagram above was between Pete Sampras and Jim Courier. Looking in the parentheses, we see that Sampras was seeded number 6 in the tournament and Courier was seeded number one. Both men are from Florida.

Now, how does tennis scoring work? The object is to win either 2 out of 3 or 3 out of 5 **sets.** Each set is made up of a number of **games.** A player needs to win at least 6 games to win a set, and he or she has to win the set by at least 2 games. For example, if Steffi Graf and Martina Navratilova are playing, and Navratilova wins 6 games to Graf's 3, she wins the set. But if she wins 6 games and Graf has won 5, then the set would have to continue until one or the other was ahead by at least 2 games.

The score in a game will be listed under the player information. Below is a box score for a matchup between Monica Seles, currently the top female player in tennis, and Jennifer Capriati, ranked fourth. Notice that Seles has her country, Yugoslavia, listed after her name because she is not from the United States.

Philadelphia Slims
YESTERDAY'S RESULTS
At Philadelphia
Singles—championship
Monica Seles (1), Yugoslavia, def. Jennifer Capriati (4), Saddlebrook, Fla., 7-5, 6-1.
Doubles—champioship
Jana Novotna, Czechoslovakia, and Larisa Savchenko, Latvia, (1) def. Mary Joe Fernandez, Miami, and Zina Garrison, Houston (4), 6-2, 6-4.

The scoring summary for the Seles-Capriati games is 7–5, 6–1. In the first set, 12 games were played before Seles won. She had to go to 7 games to beat Capriati because she needed to win by 2. The second set was easier, with Capriati only winning one game to Seles's 6.

In the case of doubles matches, where two players are on each team, the information will be given in the same way.

If a match is not played or is not completed, this will sometimes be indicated in parentheses after or instead of the score. If the match is never played (because one player is sick or injured), that player loses by default. If the match is not completed because of injury or illness, the losing player is said to have retired. For example, a match summary might read: "Ivan Lendl, Greenwich, Con., def. John McEnroe, New York (default)." This would mean that McEnroe did not play the match, and so Lendl won by default.

Some tennis matches go to **tie-breakers** if each player has 6 games. Any set that ends in a tie-breaker will have the score of the tie-breaker listed in parentheses after the set. For example, in the original example we looked at for the game between Pete Sampras and Jim Courier, the score for the second set was given as 7–6 (7–5). This tells us that both players won 6 games and the set went to a tie-breaker. In the tie-breaker, Sampras won 7–5.

INDIVIDUAL PLAYER STATISTICS

Sometimes newspapers or television commentators will use other stats for tennis players. For instance, you might see or hear about the number of **aces** a player has. An ace is any good serve in a tennis match that cannot be hit by the player's opponent, which results in a point for the server. Players with extremely fast and accurate serves tend to get a lot of aces. Some players have been known to serve the ball to their opponents at speeds in excess of 115 miles per hour.

Another serving stat you might come across is **first-serve percentage.** Players get 2 chances to serve a ball correctly. First-serve percentage measures what percentage of the time a player's first attempt at serving the ball is successful.

Sports fans also keep track of 2 statistics that have to do with the game once the serve has been successfully put into play. A **winner** is similar to an ace. It is a shot other than a serve that cannot be reached by the other player. **Unforced errors** are the flip side of winners. They occur when a player hits a ball into the net or out of bounds while attempting to return an opponent's shot. Generally, better players don't commit many unforced errors.

From the many different types of stats we have covered in this book, you can certainly see how complex and confusing the world of sports statistics can be. And new types of stats are being invented every day as people search for new ways to study their favorite sports. Using what you have learned, you should have no trouble keeping up with what's happening on the sports page or on television.

One final word about sports statistics. They don't tell us everything. In fact, there is a lot that stats *can't* tell us. They can't measure the amount of effort and determination an athlete will put into a game, for example. They can't show how much intelligence, quickness, or strength a player has, or the grace she or he exhibits while playing. While they can tell us who did what and how many times, sports statistics can never fully capture the excitement created by the women and men who actually play the games.

Index

About the Author

Jeremy R. Feinberg is the former sports editor of the *Columbia Daily Spectator* and a sportscaster for WKCR-FM. A graduate of Columbia College, he is currently a student at the Columbia University Law School. He and his brother, Doug, are avid sports fans.